▶ **Help** the kittens find their mittens.
Color the mittens red.

The 3 little kittens lost their mittens
and they began to cry.

I found _____ mittens.

A **pair** is two mittens.

I found _____ pairs of mittens.

1

Fun with Math

▶ Draw a line to make a pair.

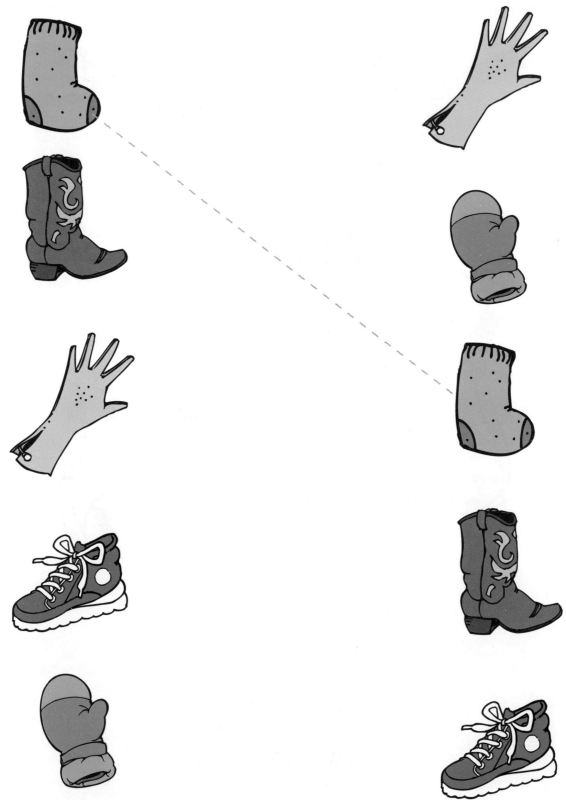

▶ Cut and glue.
Give each kitten a pair of mittens.

glue

glue

glue

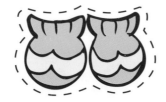

3

Fun with Math

▶ What is the number on your house?
Write it on this door.

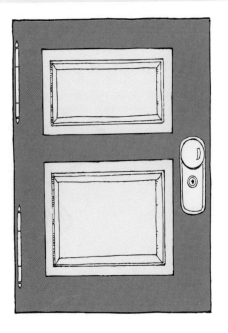

▶ What is your telephone number?
Write it in this book.

► Help Little Red Hen pick up her eggs.
Write a number on each egg.

► How many eggs did Red Hen get? _____

Fun with Math

Connect the dots. Fill in the numbers.

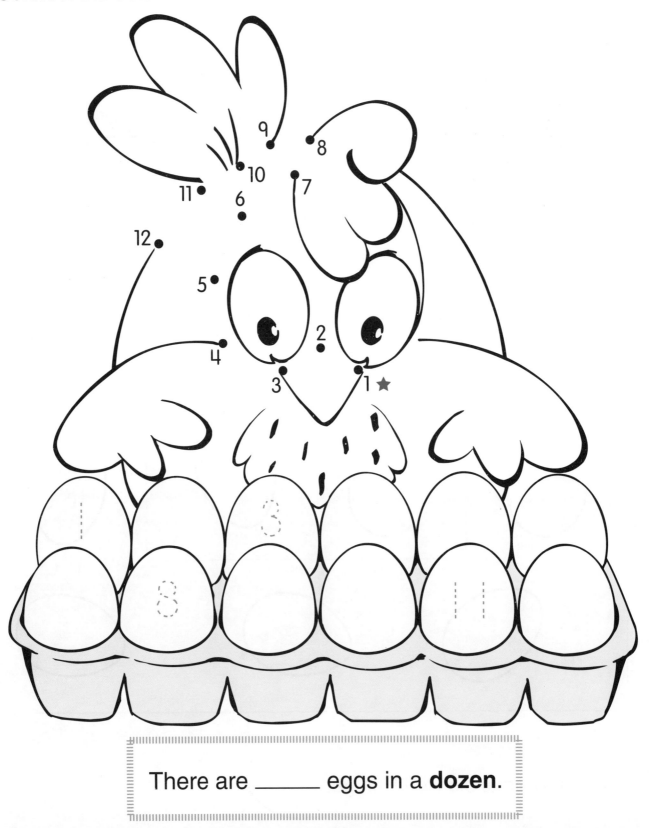

There are _____ eggs in a **dozen**.

Look at each pattern.
What comes next?

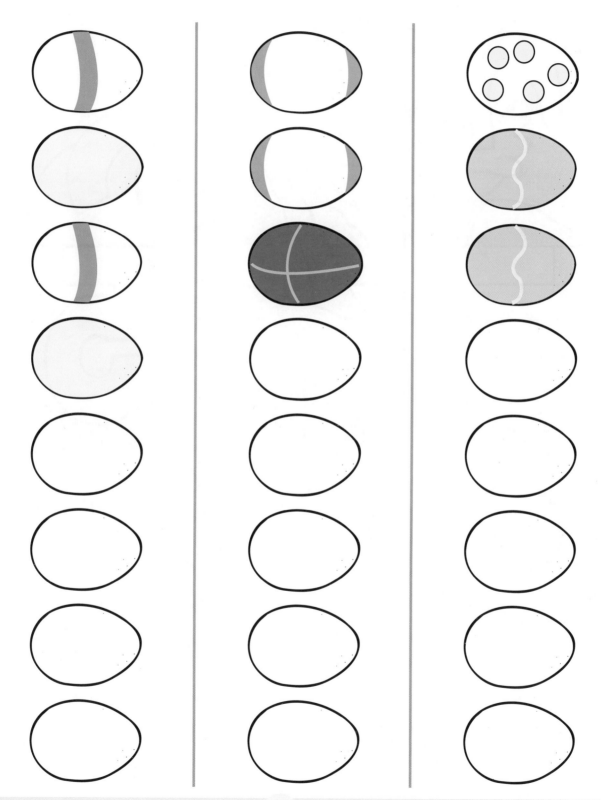

Fun with Math

▶ Find the numbers and color them.

▶ Circle the numbers you found.

0   1   2   3   4   5   6   7   8   9   10

Fun with Math

Connect the dots to find the shape. Circle the answer.

Start at **1**.

1
9
2
8
3
7
4
5
6

This is a _____.

Start at **1**.

12 11
1
10
2
9
3
8
4
7
5 6

This is a _____.

Start at **1**.

1 7
6
2
5
3 4

This is a _____.

Start at **1**.

1 13 12 11
2 10
3 9
4 8
5 6 7

This is a _____.

Fun with Math • LL 6926

Fun with Math

▶ Start at **1**.
Connect the dots.

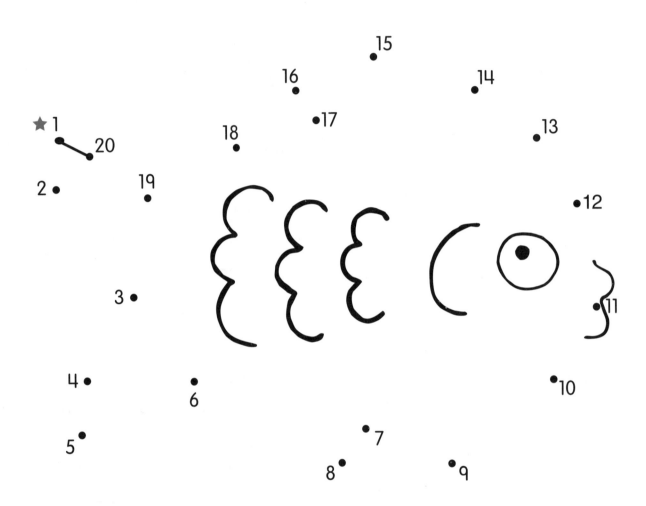

▶ What did you find?

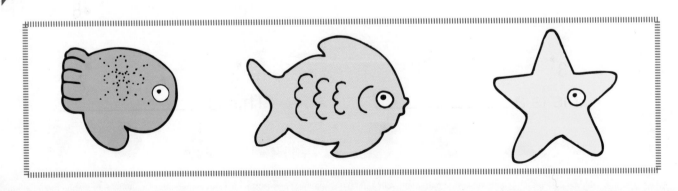

▶ Trace and color the fish.

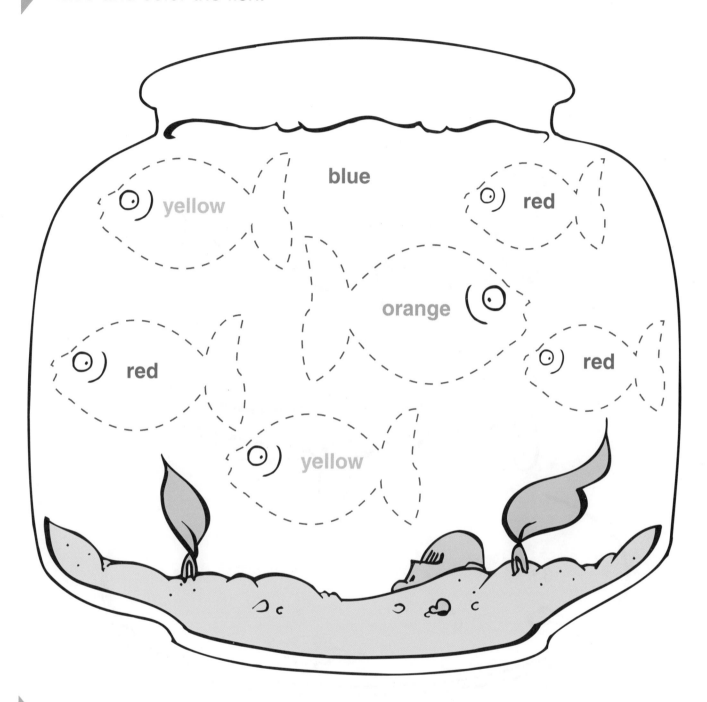

▶ Count the fish.

There are _____ fish in the bowl.

Fun with Math

▶ Start at **1**. Connect the dots.

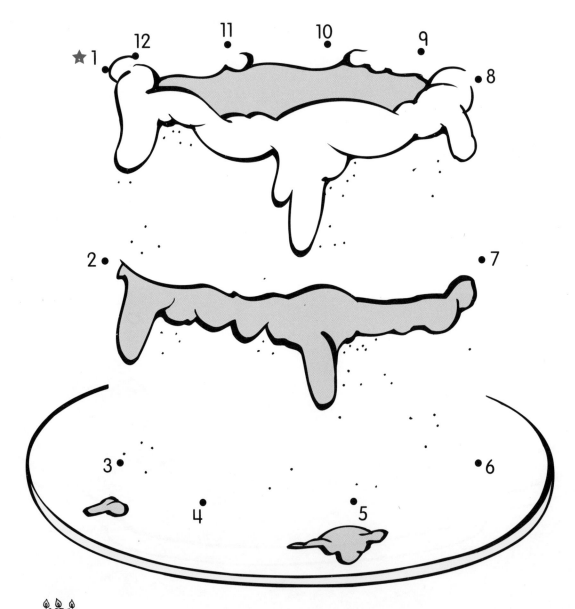

▶ Draw candles on the cake to show how old you are.

I am _____ years old.

Fun with Math • LL 6926

▶ Cut out and glue to complete the puzzle.

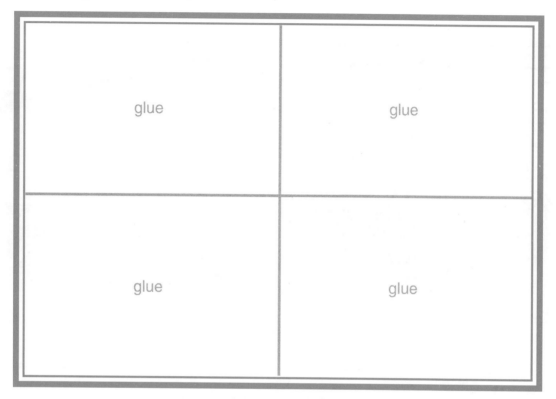

▶ How many presents do you see? _____

Fun with Math

When is your birthday? Write the date on the line.

My birthday is on:

_____
month   day   year

Help the caterpillar find its dinner.
Fill in the missing numbers.

	1	2	3	4	5	6

	26		28		7

24	41		43	30	8
23			44		9
22	39	49	45	32	10
	38		47		
	37		35	34	12

19		17	16		14

Fun with Math

▶ Color the flowers in the garden.

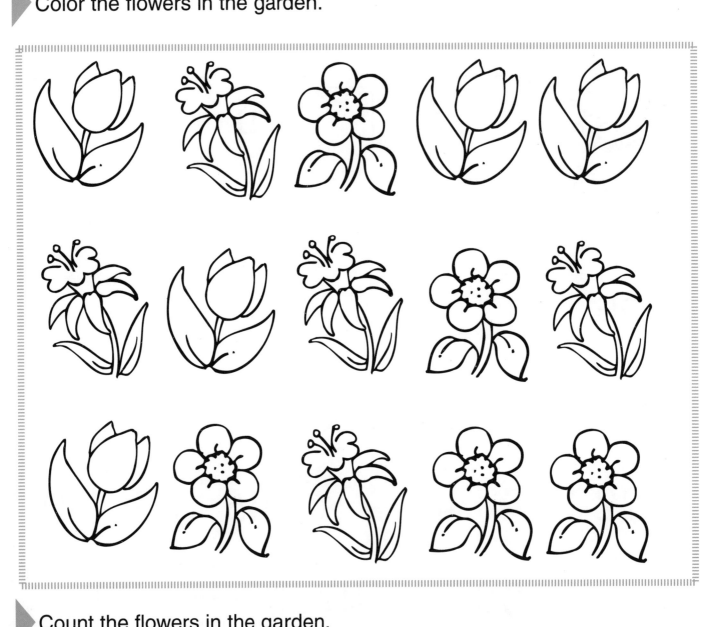

▶ Count the flowers in the garden.

There are _____ flowers in all in the garden.

Find and color the shapes in the garden.

yellow — ◯   **green** — ▭   **red** — ⬡   orange — △

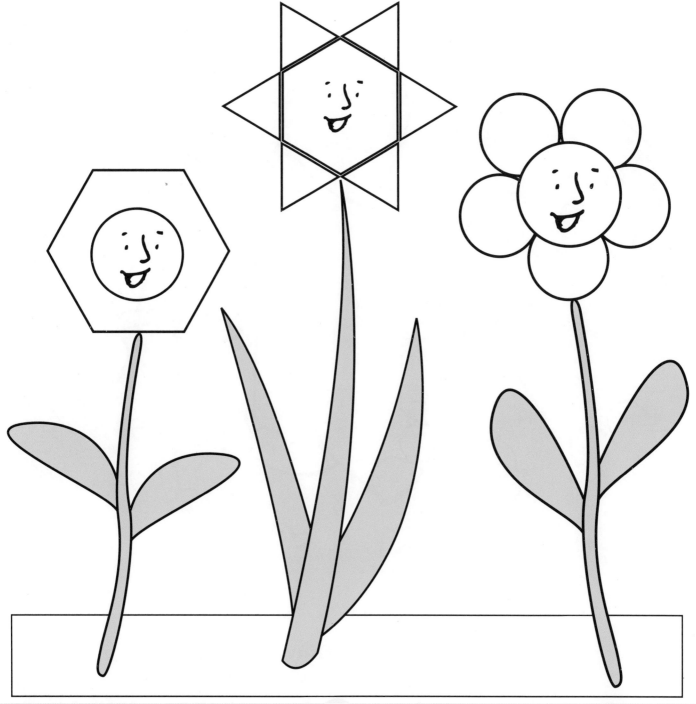

Fun with Math

Start at **1**. Connect the dots.
Who can this be?

I am big.
Color me gray.

Match each elephant to its peanut.

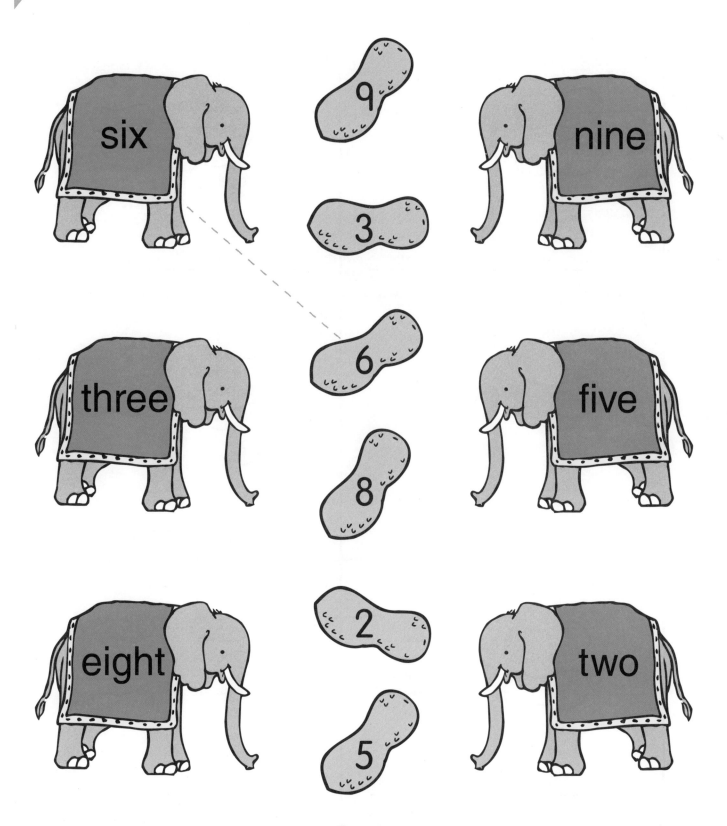

Fun with Math

 Add the peanuts to see how many the elephant gets to eat.

1.

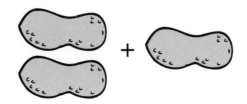

2 + 1 = 3

2.

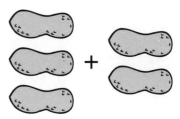

_____ + _____ = _____

3.

_____ + _____ = _____

4.

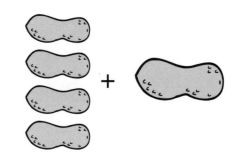

_____ + _____ = _____

5.

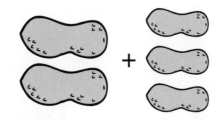

_____ + _____ = _____

6.

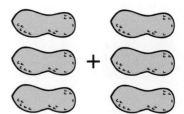

_____ + _____ = _____

The clown has lost his hat.
Connect the dots to find it for him.
Color the clown.

13

12

14

11

15   blue

10

16

17

9

18

8

★1

7

2

6

3   4   5

red

yellow

Fun with Math

▶ Color the shapes.

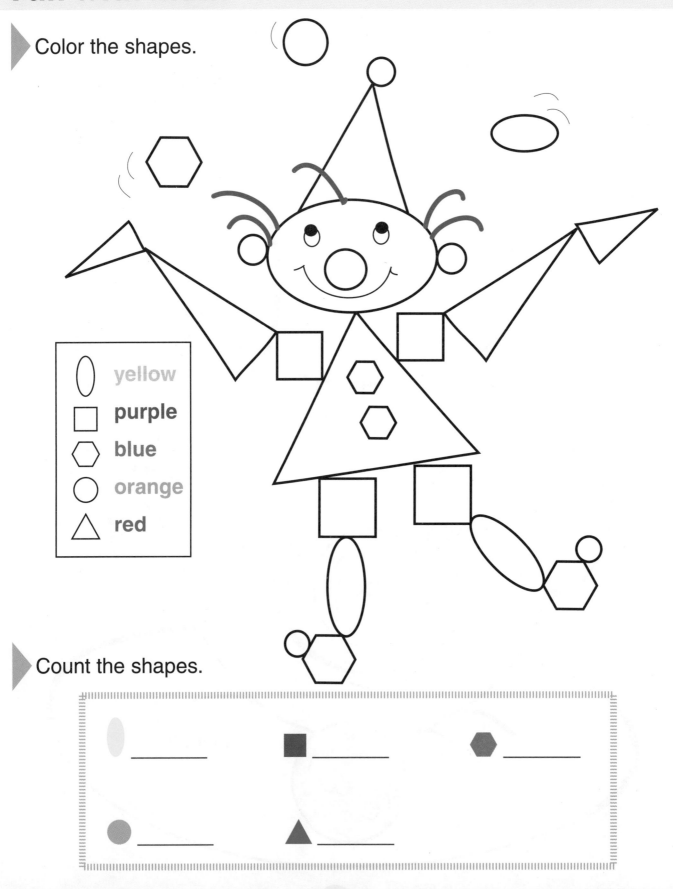

	yellow
	purple
	blue
	orange
	red

▶ Count the shapes.

first　　**second**　　**third**　　**last**

▶ Fill in the blanks.

1. This clown is

_____

in line.

2. This clown is

_____

in line.

3. This clown is

_____

in line.

4. This clown is

_____

in line.

Fun with Math • LL 6926

Fun with Math

Subtract to see how many hats are left.

1.

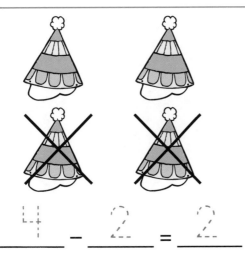

4 - 2 = 2

2.

_____ - _____ = _____

3.

_____ - _____ = _____

4.

_____ - _____ = _____

5.

_____ - _____ = _____

6.

_____ - _____ = _____

Connect the dots.

Hickory, dickory, dock.
A mouse ran up the clock.

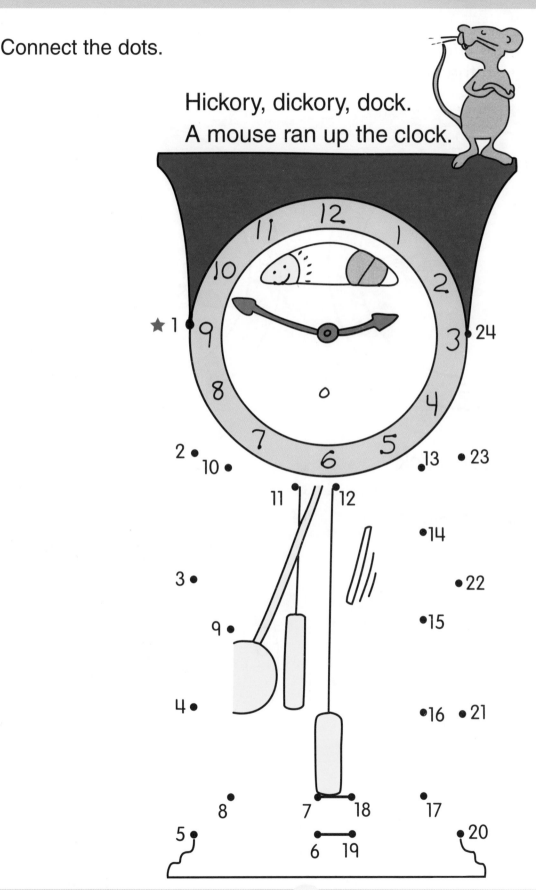

Fun with Math

What time is the little mouse showing you?
She is sitting on the hour hand.

_____ o'clock

_____ o'clock

_____ o'clock

_____ o'clock

Fun with Math • LL 6926

▶ Draw a line to match the answers.

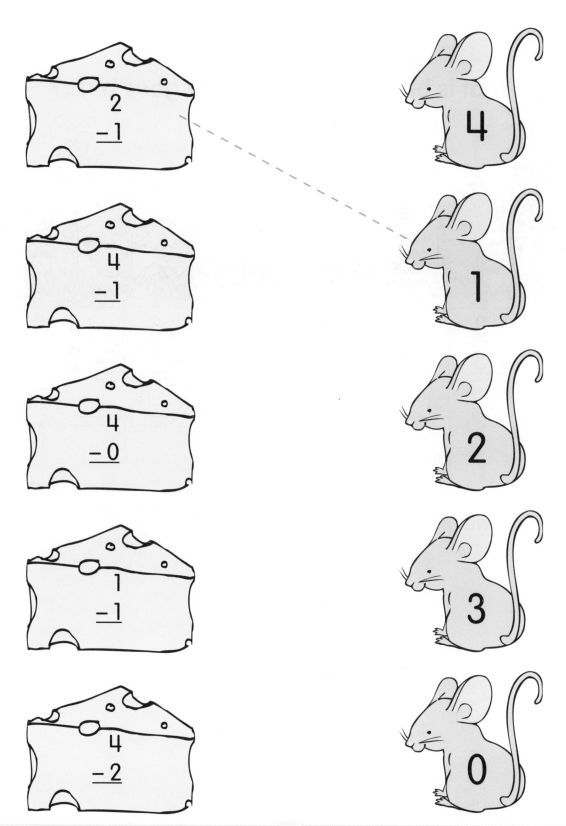

$$\begin{array}{r} 2 \\ -1 \\ \hline \end{array}$$

$$\begin{array}{r} 4 \\ -1 \\ \hline \end{array}$$

$$\begin{array}{r} 4 \\ -0 \\ \hline \end{array}$$

$$\begin{array}{r} 1 \\ -1 \\ \hline \end{array}$$

$$\begin{array}{r} 4 \\ -2 \\ \hline \end{array}$$

4

1

2

3

0

Fun with Math

Work the problems.
Look at the code.
Answer the riddle.

What is black and yellow and goes buzz?

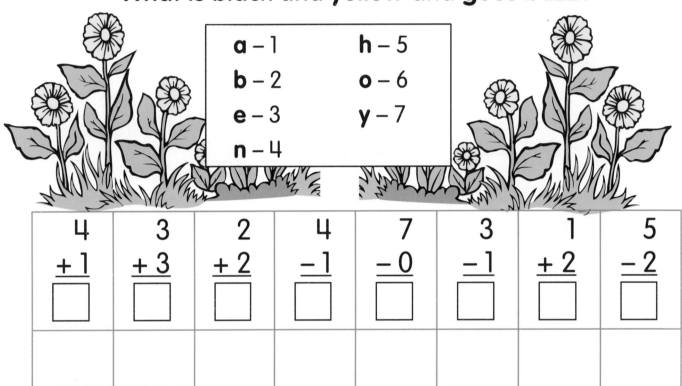

a – 1	h – 5
b – 2	o – 6
e – 3	y – 7
n – 4	

4 +1	3 +3	2 +2	4 −1	7 −0	3 −1	1 +2	5 −2
□	□	□	□	□	□	□	□

Draw the answer here.

▶ Add or subtract. Find the answers.

Answer Key

Please take time to go over the work your child has completed. Ask your child to explain what he or she has done. Praise both success and effort. If mistakes have been made, explain what the answer should have been and how to find it. Let your child know that mistakes are a part of learning. The time you spend with your child helps let him or her know you feel learning is important.

Page 1
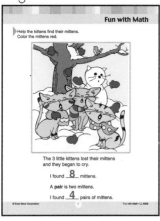

Page 2
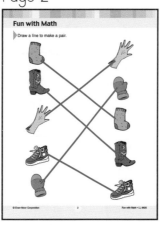

Page 3

Page 4

Page 5
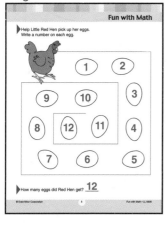

Page 6

Page 7
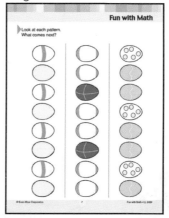

Page 8

Page 9
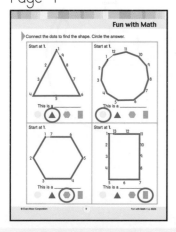

Page 10
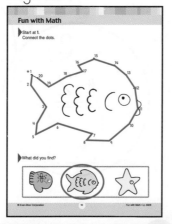

Page 11
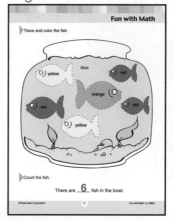

Page 12
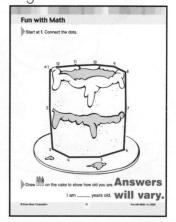

Page 13

Page 14

Page 15

Page 16

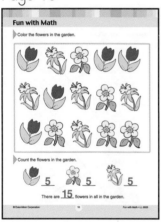

Page 17

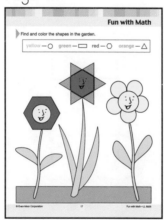

Page 18

Page 19

Page 20

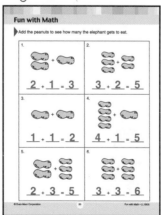

Page 21

Page 22

Page 23

Page 24

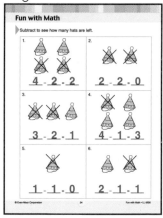

Page 25

Page 26

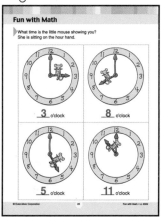

Page 27

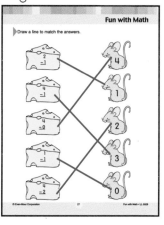

Page 28

Page 29